War Baby
Autobiography
My Early Years

War Baby
Autobiography
My Early Years

Wendy Rosaline Elcock

Published by W R Elcock

© Copyright W R Elcock 2019

WAR BABY
AUTOBIOGRAPHY
MY EARLY YEARS

ISBN 978-0-244-48318-0

Book formatted by www.bookformatting.co.uk

Contents

Acknowledgements

To my daughters Lise and Ellen and grandson Jakc. They are my inspiration to write my memoirs and some history to pass on for future generations.

In memory of John Oliver Roger Williams my dear friend and confidant.

My special thanks to Andy for his support and contribution with the book.

1

1942 – 1954

Britain was at war with Germany. It was half way through now and morale was low, London had been badly bombed and there was the usual chaos that warfare can cause. It was August 1942 and London was experiencing a mini heat wave. Despite this, my parents Margaret and Hugh Wright decided to head for the local cinema where the film Jungle Book was showing, as some light relief and distraction was needed. Mum was expecting her second child and was due any day soon. They managed to hop on the bus to reach their destination. After a while, Mum felt her waters break and she realised that she was in labour. Another hop on the bus and home quickly. The midwife who was called was a capable Irish woman who had seen it all before. On August 4th in the early hours I came into the world and a comment from the midwife stating this one has been here before! I was soon to be wrapped in a fur coat and taken into the air raid shelters when the sirens sounded for the next bombs to drop on London, we all waited for the all clear in dim dreary surroundings and hoped there was not too much devastation or loss of life close to our homes. As a baby I was totally unaware and was probably just awaiting my next feed and change of clothing. As I grew up my mother realized she had a tomboy on her hands that liked to get into scrapes and wanted to bandage her own knees and her brother's when she grew older. In a vain attempt to add a more feminine touch, my hair was styled in ringlets with a hot rod device and I wore pretty dresses for a while. John and I liked to make mud pies in the garden, climb trees and generally get messy as kids do.

Mum and Dad had met at a local dance about a year before. Mum was working at a factory for the war supplies and her friend thought it would be a good idea if they both went out for a bit of fun and light relief from the endless dreary talk of war. They put on their best frocks, let their hair down and danced the night away. Dad was in the area working as a Chartered Accountant working on audits in the local area and staying at the Black Horse Hotel. He thought she was the prettiest girl there in her yellow frock waiting for someone to ask her to dance and sipping a cool drink with her friend. She was dainty with a slim bone structure and light on her feet. He was tall and handsome with dark eyes and dark wavy hair. He was a gold medallist for Ballroom Dancing and Mum was determined to have a ball, even though she failed to mention that she was married with a son. It was only after six months into their romance that the secret was out. This did nothing to deter his passion and as a staunch Scotsman he was determined to marry her. He even tried to persuade Arthur, Mum's husband, to hurry the process of divorce along by offering a settlement of cash, which Arthur found distasteful and upsetting and would not agree to. It was all eventually settled in court.

He wrote a card to my mother with 'My Love is Like a Red Red Rose', by the poet Robert Burns - how romantic is that! This swayed my mother into leaving her first husband Arthur and with my father's persistence the poor man had little choice. He had been allocated to the coast and had been away from home as many were. He was not fit enough for active service and was given less arduous desk type work to do his bit for the war effort. He was certainly no match for my father who was a well-educated debonair man and drove his own car, which was not so common in those days, and knew exactly what he wanted and how to get it.

The only daughter of grandparents Ellen and Harry Tyler, Margaret was becoming wayward and would not listen to their advice. Mum having decided to leave Arthur and leave Anthony her son to be brought up by them. Arthur was distraught, he was to lose both his wife and son although it appears, he did not have the heart to fight, he became lonely, depressed, and never remarried. Anthony settled well with his grandparents in the small house in Kidderminster. He was a toddler aged two years a quiet reserved child and was to be a lovely addition to their life. He remained with them and after graduating from art college, eventually married Sue in the early 60's and went on to have a daughter and a son, Sarah and Steven.

Meanwhile, Mum started her new life with Dad in Harrow and Wembley two years after my birth. Mum's third child was born 30th September 1944, a boy she called John Munro. Mum had made an effort to look good after the birth though Dad failed to notice! There were already cracks starting to show in this marriage. Dad was a keen golfer and liked a whisky at the Clubhouse and was often late for family meals, this did nothing to help their relationship. The meal which was being kept warm in the oven eventually got dry and burnt and he would throw it aside in disgust onto the floor and Mum would end up in tears. He also left her short of money and left just about enough on the mantlepiece for food. When we children needed extra for clothing or shoes a row would start. This forced Mum to seek a part time job and leave us children with our Housekeeper, Mrs Sly, a drab older lady who we were not so fond of and who was just doing her duty and no more. We would escape into the garden and continue with our mud pies and digging for worms.

Events all came to a head the summer of 1948, when Mum came home from where she worked as a waitress and cook, to find her belongings scattered outside the house and all over the pavement. She was unable to have access to the house. John had accompanied Mum to work and I was still in the house with Mrs Sly. Mum insisted I came out too and eventually Mrs Sly let me out onto the pavement. Dad was nowhere to be seen and was probably with his sister, my Aunt Peggie. Mum now had a real dilemma to face as we were now all homeless! With very little money and just the clothes on our backs we trudged our way to the café where she was working. Her employer put us all up for the night but after that Mum had to find alternative accommodation for us. There had been a recommended place from her employer, a kind Jewish man, for John and I to be housed alone in care and Mum would have to leave us there.

We made our way to Teddington and John and I were placed into a private Children's Home there. I was nearly six years old and John almost four. We were greeted by Mrs Drinkwater the House Mother. She mentioned we were both bonnie children with dark eyes and rosy complexions and looking very bewildered. All I remember was the lovely garden and feeling very hungry. Mum must have left us to make a new life for herself. I don't even remember saying goodbye to her or her departure. As a young child I was totally unaware and just focused on myself and John and how we would be and hoped to adjust to a new way of life without my parents and their care. We settled in fairly well and I remember thinking I'm on my own now! Neither one of our parents appeared to want us children or fight hard enough to keep us close. Therefore, this would probably affect our wellbeing and formation of character well into adult life, time would tell. It would either break or make us, as an optimist I was determined to give it my all and hope for the best.

The home was run by Mrs Drinkwater and Mrs Head her deputy. They were both strict with a no-nonsense attitude. Although they were also kind and understanding to us children, all from broken homes, we were all able to quickly form an alliance. There were around ten young children in residence, mostly brothers and sisters, it was like coming from a large family. We had a lot of fun and, as we were all in the same boat, were able to understand that some families lived different lives. I soon became efficient in doing tasks such as peeling potatoes and darning socks which we did in the evenings. We all sat with our mushroom holders to steady the socks and neatly repair the holes. We also generally helped with household tasks. Post war was hard for many people, families with weary husbands dispersed abroad, maybe never to return and fathers and sons killed also. This put a lot of sadness and pressure on the women and made many of them self-sufficient, hardy. They needed all their wits about them to survive this difficult period. We children were put into training along these lines. It taught us values of how to be tough, kind, care and look out for each other.

The home was run like an American boot camp without the

salutes and shouting orders. A gong sounded for meal times and we all sat around a wooden table, a short grace was said by the House Mother, we had to sit up straight with elbows tucked in and practice perfect table manners. We were also expected to eat all that was put before us, there were still rations in force and fussy eating was not allowed. Meals were fairly simple, meat, mainly rabbit, or awful boiled tripe, potatoes and overcooked vegetables with some fruit to follow. We had bread and dripping for supper if we were still hungry as we always seemed to be. We had no sweets, cake or biscuits, ice cream, or all the things that children liked. One good thing, we all had good teeth and were all very slim and agile. After the meal we cleared the table and if lucky we could listen to the radio or read the comics Dandy and Beano before bedtime.

We attended the local primary school at Hampton Wick which was around a mile walk from home. Sometimes we would spot the milkman finishing his round on a cart pulled by a horse which had a leather bag of oats fitted around its neck. When the milkman dashed in and out of the various homes leaving a bottle or two on each door step, the poor horse was able to take a break and enjoy his breakfast from the feeding bag. I also passed a home for mental health disease. We as children were fascinated as we didn't fully understand and it was a mystery to us. We longed to see the residents and occasionally we did and ran away in fear! It was also my time for day-dreaming and I thought I was a fairy and looked for signs of wings growing from the scapula, with each viewing in the mirror no growth as yet. Each night I would visit fairyland under the sheet, which must have been a form of escape at the time. The home was somehow associated with The Salvation Army, where we walked to their Mission three times on a

Sunday. This was a mile or two away and we sometimes played postman's knock on the way. We never got caught as we were all very nimble and able to run fast.

   This was a fun time, there was a band with lots of singing and I learned to play the tambourine and John learned to play the cornet. We would often go out with the band onto the streets collecting for the poor and homeless. They had an enormous colourful flag which waved in the breeze and the joyful band would soon attract a passer-by or more and they would put their odd coins from their purses or pockets into our collecting box. We would give them a copy of The War Cry the newsletter from the Salvation Army. The Army wore smart uniforms – suits with golden braid for the Men and suits for the Women with a bonnet tied with a large bow under the chin. I was a Sunbeam, the equivalent of a Brownie, then a Lifesaving Guard, equivalent to a Girl Guide. We had smart uniforms too and learnt lots of useful trips for survival e.g. how to tie knots with ropes and camp cooking, also putting up basic tents. We worked in teams and each one relied on the other to do a good job, all basic training for a good adult life. I still have a soft spot for this wonderful institution which had no airs or graces, just simple basic rules to care for the less fortunate in our society.

   A real treat for us children was each Christmas Eve the band played carols outside the Home which might not have been popular with local neighbours, but I was not aware of any complaints at the time. A party was organised on Boxing Day with lots of treats and a super tea party with crackers decorated along the long table where we all sat in anticipation and with greedy appetites, tucked into this fantastic feast. On Christmas Day there was always an Orange at the bottom of our stockings and if lucky some chocolate. We played musical chairs and blind fold add the tail onto the picture of the donkey. There was plenty of giggles and fooling around as we all tried to compete with each other. The home-made Christmas pudding had sixpence pieces cooked with it and if lucky you might find one in your mouth, no health and safety rules then, no one ever choked or became ill, it was just simple fun. I don't remember Mum coming to visit very often, life must have been a struggle for her coping on her own in post war London and finding work and accommodation together. There were no letters, telephone calls or any form of communication, I just accepted this as normal and got on with my life.

On one occasion she turned up out of the blue and took John and I to the local cinema in Kingston and for tea afterwards. She always looked glamorous and well-dressed, it was hard as her visits were nice but infrequent. Mum met George in London and they became close and he helped her overcome some of the difficulties and shouldered and protected her. For the first time in ages she had help and companionship from a man that loved her. Mum and George settled on the South Coast, happy and contented. John went to live with them in a small caravan in Hordle, Hampshire. There was no room for me and John wanted to be with his mother, He never really settled and was not so outgoing as me. He had bouts of illness and was often quiet and withdrawn, whereas I always had an opinion about everything and a confidence which could be a front for fighting my corner. I was fine and comfortable in the Children's Home and did not want to be uprooted at this point. It felt like home and I had not really known any other times that had such good memories. I had made some special friends and had become independent and liked the freedom.

Each summer my Father and I would travel up to Bridge of Allan Stirlingshire to visit my grandmother, aunt, uncle and cousin Joan who was around my age. Dad drove an Austin 7 which was slow and it took 10 hours to travel on the A6. He would always stop halfway for a slap-up meal in a hotel en route. I couldn't face a meal as I often felt nauseous which was probably due to the long journey. I spent ages looking out of the window, there was no radio and Dad said very little apart from an occasional swear word at a motorist he thought was driving badly. We would arrive around ten just as the light was fading. The two weary headlights giving their last beam before the car was being garaged for the night. After a drink and a light supper, I was ready for bed, which was up three flights of stairs in the front of the house, with a glorious view of the garden at dawn and the uplifting sweet sing-song of the birds.

Grandmother's house was rather grand, it was called Mount Ivor and it was surrounded by a beautiful garden and was within walking distance to the town. There was a sweeping gravel drive and well maintained lawns and a gardener tending them. Mealtimes seemed very formal with all the best silver, crystal glasses and linen napkins which were present at each meal. We all sat around a long table on upright chairs while the Housekeeper darted in and out with the next hot dish. Conversation was polite and I probably went into my own world of make-believe and was anxious to get the meal over. Joan and I played and I remember a child's dolls house on the lower ground floor, which was the size of the room with a little kitchen, living area and bedrooms – a child's paradise! Dad came from a family of six children and was the youngest and the favourite and the most handsome although not the easiest going to get along with, he could be remote and distant and had a bit of a temper if provoked. They teased him he had been born with a silver spoon in his mouth! As a kid I just went along with it and thought it was normal, I had no loving fathers to compare with! The family were kind to me and at the time that's all that mattered. Emotions in those days were not talked about especially to children who were seen and not heard! The two weeks in Scotland passed quickly and it was a break from my routine in the home.

Before I returned back to London, I was kitted out with clothes for the year by my aunt. Joan could not understand why I needed so many clothes all at once, she was jealous at the time and didn't realize her parents could shop and provide her needs at any time. Mine would be my only set until I grew out of them and they needed to be replaced. There were no frilly dresses or petticoats, just plain skirts and sensible blouses and jumpers with a sturdy pair of shoes. A dreary coat completed the shopping spree.

On Sundays, around once a month, Dad and Aunt Peggie, Father's eldest sister, would take John and myself out for the day. We went to Box Hill and Chessington Zoo, it was a fun time. Aunt Peggie always had a supply of chocolate bars in her bag and they were a real treat for us, as sweets were in short supply for us always hungry children. We climbed the enormous hill and rolled down giggling all the way. We went on the carousel with the painted horses that turned around to music in a magical fashion, at the fun fair in the zoo. I felt happy and carefree as children should feel.

Each year our annual holiday was at Dymchurch at a holiday camp not very far from Beachy Head. There was a miniature railway which was fun to ride on. This was a great chance for us kids to run riot and have plenty of fresh air. It was there I had my first proposal of marriage from Raymond Flashman who was also a resident at the home, He had a sister called Anne who I was very fond of too. I was only nine years old. We planned that we would have six children and never be parted, it was all very romantic at the time. We giggled behind the chalets, held hands before returning to our individual beds, his with the boys' and mine with the girls' dormitory. There was a canteen where we ate and planned activities to keep us out of trouble. Sadly, our plans for the future were not to be as Raymond went off to Christ's Hospital school as a boarder. He returned once in his dashing uniform, a cape coat with a satin lining with orange socks tucked into breech trousers. He looked happy and very pleased to share his experiences of his new life with us. After that we lost touch, I have never forgotten him! First love and all that!

Also, as the holiday fell on my birthday in August, there was never a party but we had ice creams on the beach instead and donkey rides. Life couldn't get any better! I have always enjoyed reading novels and Enid Blyton was my favourite in childhood. I was a real book worm and remain so! With the famous five I was always going on some adventure, drinking lemonade and eating slices of delicious chocolate cake with them. We would pedal for miles on our bikes, camp out, light fires and cook our sausages on a fire we had made from bracken and sticks. The retriever dog Timothy would happily join us. I just loved animals and always thought we could learn a thing or two from them, we sometimes forget we are naked apes and an animal too!

When I was aged eleven years I must have taken the eleven plus examination. I could not have passed or might not have entered as I did not go to a grammar school. I was a bit of a daydreamer with an active imagination and I just know I would be OK in life despite my obvious setbacks. There was no encouragement from either parent. I think they viewed me as a bit of an idiot and may well get pregnant early and have one each year. Nothing could have been further from the truth, I was going through a religious phase and thought I might like to be a missionary or even a nun. The idea of being a wife didn't appeal at all then. I witnessed my own mother's disappointment with two behind her and that was not for me. I had learnt some of the basic skills, how to survive in this life and keep afloat. By the age of twelve I could cook, sew, knit and communicate with people which was to put me in good stead in later life. I felt I didn't really need anybody. Adults had been mostly disappointing in my early life and I just know I had to take control of my own life and destiny.

The home was near Teddington Lock, Pinewood film studio and Bushy Park which was our playground where we would make camps, cycle madly with feet on the handle bars We had total freedom and as long as we were back for meals, we did as we liked! There was a USA camp in the park at the time, probably over from war time; the American GI'S would offer us children chewing gum over the fences. This was a novelty as we had never had chewing gum before and we kept going back for more. They all had fascinating accents and reminded me of seeing cowboy films. They were friendly chatty and not so uptight as our men and boys. They called us children Honey and Kid with a wide grin on their faces and that seemed like a new language to us.

I was a fairly fit child, only experienced the normal childhood ailments of chickenpox and a dose of measles, otherwise I had a good bill of health. Any loose baby teeth which got moving we would pull out ourselves with the help of cotton around the tooth and a door swinging in the right direction – it soon came out. We must have walked miles each week as there were very few cars on the road at the time and we had no money for bus fares. If we did happen to board a bus, there was always a conductor to take our cash. He had a machine that rolled the ticket out almost like magic. He would shout out each stop and there was no excuse to get off at the wrong destination. No adult accompanied us, we were expected to leave on time and return safely on time also. We were well cared for, but the emotional tie that close families have was lacking. We just had to get along and make bonds in different ways with each other as friends do. We never really talked about how we felt coming from broken homes, only with school friends did I feel different, as divorce in those days was quite unusual. After school was over for the day, they would return to their loving families and I would go home to care in a different setting.

Life continued on as before apart from the obvious fact I was soon to become a teenager. I was not very tall and looked years younger than my age, had a bright rosy face, brunette hair with auburn lights which had a curl and wave to it. I wore it up in a ponytail and put my beret flat on the head on school days. I had inherited my Mother's delicate bone structure, with high cheek bones and a round face, I was slim with small hands and feet. I would have loved ballet lessons or to learn to play the piano. I was also mad about horses and would have loved to learn to ride. These were only pipe dreams as funds were not available and I had all that was necessary to survive. Fate was to take a dramatic turn and turn my orderly life upside down and to lead to three years of dismay and unhappiness.

2

1955 – 1957

It was decided I was to leave the Children's Home when I was almost thirteen years old. It was July 1955, School had broken up and I left the Church School in Teddington and the house which had been my home for the last seven years. Father was to remarry and I was to go to live with him, his new wife and her daughter in late October 1955. Before that I was to have my last time of freedom and feeling carefree. I went down to Hampshire with a small case on the coach to stay with Mother, John and George, Mother's third husband, for six happy weeks in their small caravan in Hordle. It was to be a bit cramped. I was given a small bunk bed at the back which folded up during the day allowing more space. There was a small main room which had a fold-back bed too for Mum and George, bed space somewhere for John also. We cooked on a minute cooker and we all needed to be orderly and tidy. Meals were eaten from a table that folded out once the main bed was fixed away.

Mother and George set off for work early each morning that left John and I able to ride our bicycles all day and generally do what we liked. I remember the sun shining each day, it was lovely to get to know Mum more again and to spend time with

John. We went the local cinema, to see 1950's musicals that were all the rage from Hollywood USA. I had a crush on Danny Kaye and Gene Kelly and would have loved to dance and sing like them. I wore a full circular skirt with a pair of green pointed winkle picker shoes and practiced my moves with music playing from an ancient record player when everyone was out and I could twirl to my hearts delight, this made me so happy! George was a Scot who liked to smoke his cigarettes on the step of the caravan, read the paper and do the pools. He was generous although they must have been short of money; he was the one that gave me the new red bicycle which I was to have for years. Despite lack of space we all got along well with no arguments or disagreements. It was Summer, the evenings were long and John and I were often out on our bicycles and would cycle for miles along the coast and in and out of woods. The washing and shower facilities were close by and that helped if caught unaware at night! There was also a local convenience store for bread, milk and vegetables and George's roll up tobacco for his smokes. The time passed too quickly, once more I was on the move and, with a small case packed, set off on the coach to the Midlands alone and wondering what life had in store for me this time.

When the new term for school began, it had been decided I would live with my grandparents and brother Anthony in Kidderminster, before eventually moving to Wembley to live with Father and his new family. Ellen and Harry were the salt of the earth, honest very hard working and lived a humble life. Their house was a modest single brick small house which could get very cold in the winter. There was only a small coal fire in the main living room which never filtered to the rest of the house.

Grandfather was a contented man, he had a clear complexion with no lines, which was surprising as he was out in his garden in all weathers. They kept hens, grew all their own vegetables, had fruit trees and made their own wine. Grandma was a very good cook and kept her food in a cold pantry, washed her clothes by hand and used an old mangle before putting them on a long washing line. I was fascinated by a blue block she added to her wash which was supposed to make the white garments brighter – she swore by it!

My bedroom was to be the front spare room downstairs which doubled up as a guest room, although not many people came to visit. There was no bathroom, just a cold lavatory off the small kitchen area; money was short so newspaper was used in the lavatory! Baths for me were to be in my front bedroom in a metal bath once a week. I did sneak down to the local baths as well for a top up. Anthony was at Art School and I didn't see much of him at the time. He was seventeen years old, rode a Norton motorbike and liked to hang out with his own friends, although I found out later one of them had a crush on me when he gave me a wooden jewellery case lined with red velvet which he had made himself. I still have it!

I attended the local school called Harry Cheshers which I cycled to on my red bike, it was a mile or two away from Grandparents' home. I was very happy staying in Kidderminster, as each Saturday morning I went to the pictures at the local cinema. They showed mostly cowboy films and some Walt Disney cartoons. I was in seventh heaven, I loved it all! Gran and Grandad would go to the library to renew their books and have a stout and crisps afterwards, their only time to indulge, I think! Sometimes I would join them, it was lemonade for me with a bag of crisps that contained a neat little blue salt packet to shake over the crisps and then blow up the bag later and make it go pop! If they felt really flush it would be a fish and chip supper to be collected from the local chippie on the way home. These were to be happy memorable thoughts for a difficult time ahead unknown to me at the time. Time passed too quickly and in mid-November I was soon to be on the move again to live in Wembley. Standing on the door step outside the small house in Kidderminster, Grandma was in tears, with Grandad and Tony doing the manly thing. I left on the train to Wembley on my own to a completely different life. How I would miss this small trio that had shown me love and affection for the first time in my life.

Father's new wife Ruby, who was also called Morag by Father and her daughter Pamela, two years younger than me, met me from the train. My bicycle would not fit into the car, so I cycled behind the slow-moving car back to the house in Wembley. The house was situated half mile from Wembley Football Stadium and when the wind was in the right direction and a match was playing, you could hear the roar of the crowd.

I was given a small bedroom at the back, which was to double up as a hairdressing saloon, as Morag worked from home as a hairdresser during the week which meant I shared the room with a large upright hair dryer and numerous combs, brushes and scissors. It also meant I had to be tidy. Pamela had a more spacious bedroom at the front and the parents had the other double one. The house was semi-detached with a small garden back and front and within walking distance of Wembley Park and Wembley Central stations. This was helpful for Dad as he did the commute to central London during the working week and the odd business trip to the Middle East. There was a major plus sign, a Collie Dog called Corrie. He was to become my only friend and companion in the Wright household. It became very obvious to me early on, I was to be tolerated and licked into shape by Morag. She had worked as a Matron in a home in Glasgow for difficult children and I think that is how she viewed me.

Pamela was her only child and was very special to her and I was to be the step-daughter, not at all special, not even in the eyes of my Father. He was newly married and wanted to look good for his wife and her child, whatever she suggested was fine by him. All the effort and child rearing were to be in Pamela's favour and I was expected to muddle by and stand on my own two feet. It began almost at once. I was told by Morag there was to be no contact with my mother, brothers or grandparents, this was my new home and I had to fit in and behave.

I was sent to the local secondary state school in Wembley, was told by Morag I was not going to get anywhere in life as it didn't really matter about my education. Pamela was to have private education and a tutor was employed to see that Pamela had the proper grades to get into Ealing High School. Father adopted Pamela as his own and I became invisible. I was miserable felt unloved and couldn't wait to leave. My skills that I learnt in early childhood were soon put into use. I did all the shopping, which in those days meant going to individual shops: the fishmonger, butcher and baker, also greengrocer and general store. I lugged wicker baskets full with my purchases the one-mile home and was promptly sent back if they were not up to scratch; talk about a dogs-body, that was an understatement!

It was very fortunate that I was strong and healthy and I liked being helpful. I often cooked Sunday roast, always washed up and put everything away. Pamela was told she had too much school homework to do therefore could not help me. I knew at the time she just wanted to be lazy and get away with it. Many a night when, with door closed, I had a precious five minutes to think, I would cry myself to sleep. I told all my troubles to Corrie and he appeared to understand my distress. We would go for long walks and I would chat to him along the route to the park. When I arrived home from school it was straight into action running up and down stairs with wet towels from the hair dressing, cups of tea for any customers, peeling potatoes for the evening meal, with any luck I could read a book before bed time. I was a real book worm and could daydream how to escape my present situation. They had a small television and I often raced home to watch Dr Kildare starring Richard Chamberlain, the handsome lead doctor, when I could. If any of my readers recall Cinderella, they will get the picture! Although at that time I was not looking for a Prince, and attending a ball was out of the question as I had to finish my chores first!

Each Sunday we attended The Scottish Presbyterian Church, the parents and Pamela drove in my Father's Black Austin. I preferred to walk, it was time for more daydreaming also watch the local Teddy Boys, who hung around the coffee bars that were just about cropping up then in Wembley Central. The local Minister was a cheerful Irish Man and he made the service bearable. It was during the sermon I first saw and felt the presence of a ghost, a shimmering figure that stood beside me briefly then disappeared. It left me with a feeling of peace and hope to carry on. The church service was so different from the Salvation Army, it all seemed so formal with no joyful band just the dreary organ and the congregation singing the hymns with a collection to follow on the way out. Bless him, the friendly Minister did his best to keep us all God fearing!

The Minister also ran a local youth club at the church hall, we mostly played table tennis and I became quite good at it. I was even selected to play in a mixed doubles competition which was good for the ego. This was a time also to meet some boys having two brothers and boys in the Home, I got on with them really well as friends. One particular one, called Michael, walked me home to the gate and waved goodbye until I reached the front door. We would chat and it was lovely to have a friend that liked me, after all the hostility at home.

Another good thing was that Aunt Peggie and Uncle David lived in an apartment directly opposite Wembley Stadium just over the hill from our house. Each Saturday evening, I would escape there and eat chocolate biscuits with the gas fire on in the winter and watch TV on a tiny screen, while Uncle watched the football results. I would read a large encyclopaedia which was printed in bright colours and hoped the football would be over soon. On the mantelpiece there were large Toby jugs and lovely pictures on the walls, it all looked very homely and comfortable and I adored being there.

I loved Aunt Peggie and wished she was my Mother. She had no children of her own and she saved my sanity with my time spent in Wembley with her kindness and understanding, She was not really tactile although I know she was fond of me. It was around this time that Uncle David was run over and killed on his way home from The Green Man pub. He was fond of his drink and must have staggered into the road. Details to me as a child were not forthcoming. I do remember Aunt Peggie appeared to carry on as normal, although I didn't really know how she was, as this was never discussed. If I had been aware or realised, I would have given her a big hug and told her how much I loved her. My red bicycle was a life saver, at the weekends and holidays I would cycle to Heathrow Airport and watch the planes which I found fascinating. They were landing and taking off and I wished I could board one and escape to another land faraway!

Pamela set off to school in her smart uniform and boater and I was made into a prefect and pinned on my shiny badge to the blazer with white shirt and tie which I knotted into a Winston Knot which was trendy at the time. I was given some responsibility to set an example to my fellow schoolmates. We were a mixed bunch of boys and girls, some from different ethnic backgrounds and generally we got on. It was around this time that the O level exams were looming, I was meant to sit Biology, English, Maths and Needlework. My heart was not really in it and I had no encouragement from my parents. I would sometimes skip classes in the afternoon and go to the park with friends as school was boring! I did take Needlework and made a stiff lace petticoat with a scallop edging which was all the fashion at the time. We made a small garment on a sewing machine and I was given a book as a prize. In Domestic Science my victoria sponge cake was approved by the Head Master which I took to his office for the staff to have with their afternoon tea break.

As I was one of the youngest in my class, it was discussed that I should take more exams next year. The thought of staying on in Wembley with my unhappy home situation, I decided I would leave and hope for the best. I managed to save a little pocket money with baby-sitting for a Jewish family that owned a delicatessen and worked late some evenings. They lived next door, it was very convenient and they paid me the priceless sum of two shillings, a small fortune to me, just for looking after their two children, which I enjoyed.

I mentioned to Morag I wanted to be a nurse and her reply was God help the patients. This did not discourage me as it helped to spur me on. An interview was arranged at Edgware General Hospital with the Matron; she was a kind, sympathetic woman and seemed to understand my needs. She said it was customary to have the necessary examinations, at least five O levels, to start to train as a Registered Nurse. In my case I could sit the Hospital Entrance Examination which was Maths, English and an IQ test. I passed with flying colours and was told by the Matron I had an extremely high IQ. She must have sensed some potential as she said I could train at the hospital. I would be eternally grateful for her empathy and compassion.

It was decided I could start as a Nursing Cadet and be resident in Hampstead, starting in September 1958. I was coming up to my sixteenth birthday and could not start my training until eighteen. I left Wembley and my miserable life there to start a new chapter and an adventure. I had a small amount of savings to tide me over and I was over the moon!

Mum on holiday in Wales 1936

Dad in Malaysia 1938

Anthony aged 18 months in 1938

Mum and Dad and me as a baby 1942

Friend Goss, Dad and Aunt Peggie in Wembley 1944

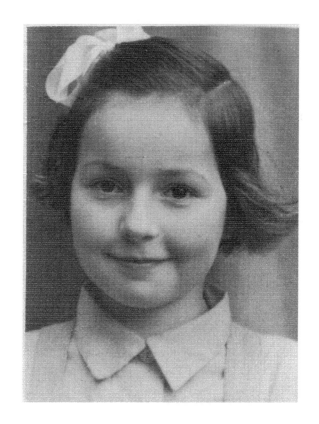

My school photograph 1947

John and myself on day out at Chessington Zoo in 1952

John first time on horseback, Chessington Zoo 1952

Anthony and school friend 1954

Mum and George in caravan at Hordle, Hampshire in 1955

Gwen with sister-in-law Hilda and brother-in-law Cyril on
leave from Nigeria with African Grey Parrots Fred and
Splinter in Wimborne, Dorset

Nursing Training School at Speden Towers, Hampstead in September 1960. I am 2nd from the left with Sylvia sitting on the rail

**Me outside Nursing Home after visiting Andrew's
Grandmother**

**Me leaning on old Ford Popular car on camping holiday in
Cornwall**

Another shot of me relaxing in Cornwall.

Meal prep at side of road, it can get hot in that old car!

Upgrade to Volkswagen, now driving in1968

Andrew, myself and nephew Robert in Wimborne 1968

Andrew on holiday in Cornwall, great swimmer and loved surfing

Grandfather Harry, Grandmother Ellen, Susan sister-in-law, Grandma's sister Winifred and her husband in Kidderminster 1970

3

1958 - 1963

My new home in Hampstead was a large house, next door to Hugh Gaitskell, Member of Parliament. It was opposite a small Catholic church with a leafy lined road which led down to a small churchyard. Many celebrities were buried here as it was quite a wealthy area and secluded from the main roads. Hampstead was to become a very trendy place to live with the Swinging Sixties just around the corner; it was also just up the hill from Hampstead tube station, very convenient to travel on the Northern Line to Edgware or into central London. It had a small cinema that showed mostly French Films with subtitles, with a dim lit cool coffee bar which were cropping up all over London. There was of course the Heath for a nice walk on a good day, sheer heaven as I was free again and able to make my own decisions.

My new friends and colleagues were all around sixteen too and we were to train as Nursing Cadets. We were supplied with smart striped dresses, an apron and a butterfly cap, which we had to learn how to assemble. We slept four to a bedroom in small single beds. We were expected to keep the rooms tidy and clean and wash our linen in the large basement down stairs.

All meals were supplied and board and lodging were to be deducted from our small pay packet. Each week day from 8.30 to 16.30 we worked in different wards and departments at Edgware General Hospital. We had our meals in the dining canteen with all the staff and there was a small sitting room for us to rest for a while afterwards. We were collected and returned back with a driver in a utility van that we nicknamed Tilly.

My first place to work was the linen room along with another cadet called Janet. It was situated directly opposite the Maternity Unit and even then, I was fascinated by the comings and goings of the pregnant women and their babies. Each morning on arrival at the linen room, we spent ages folding sheets and checking for holes and stains. We then stacked a large trolley with all the wards' linen that would be needed and headed off to stack the shelves in the various wards. There was a lot of walking up and down long corridors which was quite daunting at first, but after a while it all became very familiar.

I spent three months there and overall enjoyed the experience. It helped that there were two handsome Irish porters who worked from their office and they would often joke with us. In those days I was prone to blushing and already had rosy cheeks, I must have looked like a tomato! They flirted with us and winked and generally fooled around; it was all just a bit of fun for them and a new experience for us sixteen-year olds.

When I was seventeen, I was asked on a date by Paddy although I fancied Jimmy more, he was quieter with a mop of blondish hair and blue eyes. It was Saint Patricks Day and Paddy and I went to Café de Paris where we went dancing. He was tall with dark hair, dark blue eyes and a lot of Irish charm and we had a good time. It was all so innocent in those days and he escorted me safely back home like a true gentleman. Nothing came of it and that was my only date with him.

After working in the linen room, the next place was much more of a challenge, it was to be the Haematology Lab which tested blood samples from all over the hospital. Due to my keen approach to work and learning new skills, I was given the task of testing haemoglobin levels from samples from the patients using a special machine. The lab was opposite the mortuary and it was also my job to be given the unpleasant task to collect brain, to be ground into powder for prothrombin levels in the blood. I had a bit of a crush on the pathologist, a man probably in his thirties with blond hair and an air of superman as he knew his work inside out. I guess I didn't even exist as I was just another member of the work force. As a teenager these phases are short lived and I moved on once I left working in the lab. How fickle is youth, you think you will live for ever and death is something that happens to others, even though I had faced it head on!

My next post was the children's ward, which had a dragon of a Ward Sister in charge who ruled the ward with a rod of iron along with a staff nurse who was more approachable. The Ward Sister dished out the meals from a large heated trolley for the sick children. We were told we had to make sure they ate every morsel and came back with empty plates. These poor kids were sick with little or no appetites; I tried to make a game to it and line them up and see who could manage the most. If the plates still had food on them, I soon became adept at disposing of any waste before returning the empty plates to Sister. Each evening the children were tucked into their beds so tightly by 'The Dragon' they were terrified to move. The feeds for the babies were made up in the milk kitchen and we were allocated to feed the ones making slow recoveries and the Ward Sister tackled the really sick ones. Parents in those days were encouraged to visit only during visiting times, it must have been very distressing for them. Death was difficult to face for both parents and staff, unfortunately this would happen and it particularly upset me with older children as their personality and character were forming and they were thankfully innocently unaware. It was generally a good experience tinged with sadness, hope and joy.

I made a friend of an Irish girl called Kathleen who was a devout catholic and as the church was opposite our residence in Hampstead, she didn't have far to go to pray. We had a hitch-hiking holiday in Dublin and stayed in Youth Hostels on the way from the Ferry Port. We walked miles and I lost several pounds in weight as our diet was poor too. All I can remember eating was knickerbocker glories from a tall glass. I was already small and slight in those days but still managed to keep up. We visited Dublin and went by horse driven cart to Trinity College and the Guinness Brewery where we sampled the amber ale. I'm sensitive to alcohol so it was only a small sip for me.

We enjoyed our trip to the Emerald Isle so much, Kathleen became homesick and didn't continue to start her nurse training. I missed her and wished her well. I was the only one out of our small group who was to continue to start our general training as Registered Nurses in September 1960. I was just eighteen years old and full of hope to have a bright future.

We started our General Nurse training September 5th 1960. We were to live in a very grand house called Speden Towers, a short walk from White Stone Pond in Hampstead which was like my second home now. I already had one friend called Sylvia Tregarthen who had been living at home with her parents and five sisters in Edgware. It was the first time she had left home, although it was only for three months for our preliminary training.

We were a mixed bunch of trainees from all over the World including the Seychelles, a country we had never heard of. The man from the Seychelles was a friendly young man with a lovely smile. There were a group of girls from Malaya as it was called then, we soon made friends with them, they had beautiful olive skin and seemed exotic to us pale English. There were African, French and Caribbean and at least ten male nurses.

We were all allocated rooms which slept four to a room, each had a simple single bed and an en-suite bathroom, I had a room with Sylvia and two Malay girls. We were responsible to keep our room clean and tidy, all meals were provided and board and lodging taken out from our small pay-packet.

We were supplied with pale blue dresses, stiff white collars kept in place with a stud, white starched aprons and a starched cap and we had to wear sensible black shoes. We had a laundry box which we sent off each week for fresh supplies, we were also supplied with a black cape with a red lining for cooler days. I proudly pinned my fob watch with a second hand onto my uniform and felt I was made for this moment.

We soon fitted into the daily routine, it was like being back at school really. We sat at desks in a classroom, there was a skeleton in full view and we nick-named him Jimmy. We were expected to learn every bone in the human body, then the muscles and their attachments before we became familiar with physiology. I imagined I suffered from each new illness including diabetes, heart disease and the more I learnt the more I had! Somehow, I survived them all and soon learnt not to be so sensitive.

I was fortunate that I had already studied biology at school and had also worked with the Red Cross and had a first aid certificate. Some of the information was coming back and I was determined to do well. As a joke, we would sometimes put Jimmy in each other's beds, we had to be careful in case we got caught.

We had a document note book which was signed when we became proficient at all the learning skills we needed before letting us loose on to the wards. We had to learn all the theatre instruments for a basic theatre list in those days, they were all sterilised in an autoclave, today they are all pre-packed. We practiced giving injections into oranges and were taught how to pass a Ryle's tube into the stomach, testing urine, taking blood pressure and bandaging each other. There were sad aspects such as how to administer last rights in a dignified way, which I was soon to put into practice on my first placement when faced with death on my first allocated ward.

At the end of the three months in preliminary training, we took a written and practical exam and it was heads down to study and pass. Before the big day, Sylvia and I decided we needed a break from the books and headed off to a dance at the Police Training Cadet School at Hendon. We had a good time and made it back in time to take the exams the next day. We passed although at least fifteen failed and were asked to leave. There were no second chances in those days, which seemed pretty harsh for those leaving.

It was now time to leave Hampstead for a short while and have a small single room in the Nurses' Home at Edgware

General Hospital. Sylvia went back to live with her family as they lived near the hospital. I suddenly felt quite alone again, but there would be little time for sorrow as we were about to start shifts on the wards as a very junior probationer.

My allocation was to be the Female Geriatric Ward with thirty beds with the average age around 85 years old. It was very fortunate I loved old people and enjoyed looking after them, in some ways they had almost returned to childhood and simple tasks gave them pleasure. It was also jolly hard work, as most of them had dementia and needed round the clock care to keep them safe and comfortable. We needed to help feed, dress and help them, then get them out of bed on a daily basis. Some had stories to tell which they remembered from their past, but none could remember the day of the week or where they were. Visitors were scarce for these old ladies and this made me feel so sad, as age seemed a burden and nobody wanted to know you or love you anymore.

There were soiled beds and my job as a junior was to take all the dirty linen to the sluice and wash it down, before putting it in to bags for the laundry department to collect, you needed a strong stomach and a cheerful disposition for these tasks. My other duties were last offices for the dead which happened on a regular basis owing to my patients in a very old age group. There were frequent changes of beds and some of my old ladies liked to sit out of bed for meals. I became fond of them and did my best to keep them comfortable and safe.

I spent my first Christmas Day on the ward and we were expected to work twelve hours until the night staff came on. The Christmas decorations were only allowed up for twenty-four hours and promptly removed on Boxing Day! It was all back to normal with the daily task of bedmaking, keeping the patients clean and fed and the ward in order.

We changed wards every three months in our first year, with spells of six weeks as study in the class room. I was to work next in the operating theatre, eye unit and female surgical ward. All very challenging especially the eye theatre where I nearly fainted when I saw donor eyes ready to use in a kidney dish, I was allowed to leave for a glass of water. The Theatre Sister would not tolerate wimps so I had to return and watch each intricate procedure without batting an eye!

In the summer of 1961, Sylvia and a girl called Maureen and I decided to head for a well overdue holiday to Jersey, Channel Islands by plane. We stayed in a bed and breakfast with a charming family. After a hearty cooked breakfast, we set off to the beach to top up our tans, enjoy what we called a wet lunch in a local pub with some boys that were also on holiday and we tagged along with them for some of the time.

We had glorious weather, the sun shone every day and we all became as brown as berries. It was all an innocent fun time and a break from the hospital routine. Jersey is a beautiful Island and it was occupied during the second world war. There is a war museum and bunkers and the very pretty Jersey cows which produce the best milk ever! Time passed too quickly and before we knew it, we would be back to start our second-year training.

We were expected to do a spell of night duty for three months. My ward allocation was the Male Medical Ward and thankfully I could spend time back in Hampstead. It was quieter here so sleep during the day was more likely. It was a daunting experience on the ward, I was responsible and in charge of the ward with another junior. A male nurse from the Caribbean, he was easy going. We got on well and shared the work schedule sensibly. The Night Sister did her evening round and could be contacted in an emergency or for any advice. The work load was heavy and there were at least seven deaths each night. These were mainly heart attacks and strokes on relatively young men, I found it quite distressing as I was just nineteen years old. The duty doctor was called on each occasion to confirm the death and write out the death certificate. There were also tearful relatives to comfort, make tea for them, then the lonely task of collecting their belongings, which must have been so final and distressing for them. On the bright side most of the men were generally cheerful and I made them tea before bed. We should have given them milky drinks cocoa or Horlicks, they didn't want these as they had tea to drink at home. Total disapproval from the Night Sister had it leaked out!

Following this, I was moved to the General Operating Theatre, where you worked as part of the team picking up bloody swabs and counting them afterwards to make sure none were left inside. Theatre lists were long and often you spent all day there with just a short break. We wore cloth surgical masks and green scrubs with white boots and a frequent change of surgical gloves. You might be asked to assist and that is where you needed to know the surgical instruments. I also worked on the general surgical ward, which consisted of changing numerous dressings, removing stitches, caring for IV fluids and blood transfusions. The patients were often sick and recovery could be slow depending on the severity of their operation and some stayed in for ages. With more exams looming, I was given a purple second year belt to wear around my then 22inch waist.

In late July 1961, Sylvia persuaded me to attend a dance at

Guy's Hospital on a Saturday evening. We both looked tanned and glowing with health after our holiday in Jersey. I was not so keen and agreed to go along with her as she was looking forward to meeting a medic. Little did I know my life was to change for good as I met my future husband there.

I was wearing a blue floral dress which looked good with my tan. While we were dancing we talked. He thought I was a secretary and I thought he might be a medical student. We were both wrong, he was in his final year at Kings College London University studying Civil Engineering and had won a purple for outstanding swimming there. He was shy and handsome although dancing was not a natural movement for him, we did a shuffle of sorts and tried not to step on each other's toes.

We were poles apart in our upbringing and education. His father had worked in Trinidad and Nigeria as an engineer in the Diplomatic Service. George Andrew, their youngest, was sent to Kings School Canterbury as a boarder aged thirteen years old. He made a yearly visit in the summer holidays to see them. He was over six feet with dark hair the same colour as mine and dark smoky blue eyes and had broad shoulders which is known for athletes good at swimming. We did have our natural intelligence and independence in common. He had a dry sense of humour and made me smile.

Our first date was in Yew Gardens and we held hands in the hot house. Afterwards he took me home on the back of his scooter. We both lived in Hampstead, he was renting a small room in a large family house and I was at the Nurses, Home in Holly Walk. I was coming up to 19 and he was 22 years old, in his final year at university and I was in my second year of training. We soon became an item and managed to see each other as much as possible.

My work and studies took up a lot of time with spells of night duty and long unsociable hours. He was studying for his final exams and was also in the swimming team for the university. I would sometimes watch and check his progress with a stop watch and cheer with all the others if he came first.

In 1961, Andrew's parents settled back in the UK from Nigeria. They rented a house in Belsize Park along with their two African grey parrots called Fred and Splinter. I was taken along to meet them for afternoon tea in the garden. Robert their first grandchild was there also, asleep in his pram. He was only around a month old with blond hair and a lovely face. He was the son of Denise, Andrew's sister.

Denise was unmarried at the time and Robert's father was thought to be German. The Grandparents were to be involved with Robert's upbringing. Gwen and Edgar were Andrew's parents' names, they also had an older son called Peter who was working in design in London and was very friendly with Shirley Conran the fashion designer. They had been at Architectural College together and had become firm friends and would remain so for life.

Soon after meeting Gwen and Edgar, they moved to a rented flat in Ridgemount Gardens near Russell Square in London. Gwen was very interested in ballet and Edgar disapproved due to his religious Baptist upbringing. When I got to know Gwen better, we used to sneak to a matinee and no one was any wiser.

Andrew and my romance continued, during my second year of nursing he proposed marriage on bended knee in his parent's flat in London. I accepted and he gave me a diamond and sapphire engagement ring from a small jeweller in Edgware and a bunch of Red Roses. I was not allowed to wear the ring at work, though I wanted to as I was thrilled to bits.

We had a few ups and downs. He was about to start his first job as a Junior Engineer in Canvey Island where he stayed in rented accommodation during the week. I was working hard and preparing for my final exams. We managed to see each other as much as possible and I had to return to the Nurses' Home at a decent hour, which meant going through emergency and accident department undetected to a back staircase and a long corridor.

In November 1963, a brown envelope arrived telling me I could now practice as a registered nurse, what a joy and relief as I was just made for this vocation. I spent the next four months working as a staff nurse on a general ward before applying to start my training for midwifery.

4

1964 - 1970

1964 is the year for big changes and challenges. Firstly, I was a reluctant bridesmaid to Pamela who had a quick wedding a few months earlier due to an unexpected pregnancy. The wedding was at the Presbyterian Church in Wembley Central and conducted by our Irish Minister. Pamela looked lovely and carried a large bouquet of Arum-lilies. I wore a long apricot dress with a flower in my hair. There was a modest reception at a local hotel to follow. The next day I went back to work and the happy couple went on honeymoon. Pamela had a lovely daughter in May, 1964, she called Fiona. John, Pamela's new husband was a man a few years older and he had been the youth club leader at the church in Wembley. They moved to live in Norfolk after the wedding and I didn't see much of them.

In January, I started my midwifery training at St Stephen's Hospital in Chelsea. It was going to be a tough six months as we were expected to work full time and study as well. I shared a room with a girl who had trained at Guy's Hospital. We soon become friendly with two girls from Rhodesia as it was known then. All four of us got along so well that after our training we had a lovely relaxed holiday in Cornwall before both my Rhodesian friends returned home to practice their skills in their homeland, meet husbands and have babies of their own.

During our course, we witnessed ten normal births before we were allowed to deliver any babies with supervision from our midwife. We were in fierce competition with medical students as it was a training hospital for medics too. It was all very daunting and so different from general medicine. The midwife appeared to have so much responsibility and although child birth is a normal process, events can turn horribly wrong at short notice. This is the time the midwife would seek medical aid and was well trained to deal with medical emergencies. Otherwise normal child birth was conducted solely by the midwife for a healthy outcome for mother and baby.

My first delivery was on 20th February 1964 – what a whopper! A healthy 11lb boy all slippery and covered in a white substance which allows the birth easier for mum and baby. After that first exhilarating experience, I went on to deliver 50 normal births. I seemed to be in the right place at the right time. We were often very tired, as after a spell of twelve hours working we were expected to attend lectures until eleven. Then be on duty ready for action the same night, this job was not for the faint hearted.

It was not surprising I failed the exam and had to retake two months later which I then passed. It was also at this time I was having a rocky time with my courtship. Andrew appeared reluctant to set a date for our marriage. I was also getting pressure from Morag who had not taken to Andrew and said I would be a lap dog all my life if I married him. After completing my first six months, I had some serious thinking to do regarding the future; plans were not going well and I did not want a man in my life that was not fully committed to me. His indecisive behaviour held up red flags and I thought it was time for me to back off until he came to his senses and know what he really wanted.

I then made a decision to return his ring and continue with my general training as a staff nurse in Glasgow. I was upset at the time but proud and determined to have all or nothing. Sylvia was training there as a student midwife and I applied to the same hospital and started working there and shared a room with her. It had two single beds and as Sylvia was working nights and I worked day shifts it worked out well. I ate at the hospital and had a bath in the changing area where I left my uniform in a locker. Alcohol consumption was a problem in Glasgow and it was common to see a man drunk lying on the pavement oblivious to his surroundings and unable to make it home, until the effects wore off and he was able to stagger back. There was a funny little underground train system that only took tokens as payment for travelling on it. The men all spat on the buses and there was a fierce rivalry with the two football teams Celtic and Rangers; any excuse for a punch up with the opposing team if they lost. Men appeared rough and tough, but they were also genuine and hardworking and brought the bacon home for their wives!

I was not in contact with Andrew. Apart from a message to tell me his grandmother had died and he was missing me. I was not going to be easy going and delayed meeting until I was ready. I had to fly back to London to re-sit a midwifery exam and was greeted by delighted Andrew with a large bunch of flowers. That's more like it I thought! The time apart had made up his mind and we began to plan our wedding for March,

1965. We chose an eighteen-carat wedding ring which had simple engraving on its wide band, from a jeweller in Oxford Street. I was like a cat with two tails, it was all so exciting! I resat my midwifery exam and thankfully passed despite all the distractions.

The time spent in Glasgow was delightful as the patients were mainly from the Gorbals and when rehomed they still wanted to keep their coal in the bath as was their custom. They all had strong accents and called me the posh little girl from London. When admitted to the ward as inpatients, they all received a flea bath as some came in with bites and scratching and we could not contaminate the other patients or staff. They were good humoured about it and happy just to sink into the warm water and use a clean fresh towel. It was the first time I had witnessed poverty at close range and although they had very little, they appeared content. We also had to be aware the odd cigarette was not smoked under the bed covers as some were bed-bound and craved their smokes. I would wheel some out away from the ward to indulge in their habit. It seemed to work as we got along so well and they saved to give me a wedding present when I left to marry and work in London.

I wanted to be nearer the flat where Andrew was living with his parents. I managed to get a job as a staff nurse at The National Hospital in Queens Square which had accommodation as well. The hospital was the world expert in neurological diseases and it was a great place to work. All the food came up to the ward on silver platters and looked tasty for an NHS hospital which normally serves very bland food, a blob of potato with runny mince or pale fish and a jelly or blancmange to follow, all washed down with tepid tea. One of the consultants there was the four-minute mile record holder Roger

Bannister. I became expert at dealing with epileptic fits, patients with Parkinsons, and very sad cases of young men with Motor Neurone Disease. Huge research programmes took place at this hospital for neurology and there was a scary lab in the basement for this work to take place, which I avoided. I was also planning my wedding for March and planned to hire a beautiful ivory gown made of wild silk, which on my small budget I would never be able to buy outright. It was long, elegant and I thought looked like a million dollars, after all you don't do this every day and it was my first chance to live in wonderland, if only for a few hours. A pair of satin stiletto high heels and a raised veil completed my outfit for my long-awaited wedding.

1965 – My marriage, new home and new life. The big day had arrived, Dad and Morag had moved from Wembley to live in Seer Green in Bucks. I stayed there for a week with them prior to the wedding day. I had a cold so took it fairly easy and just took Corrie out in the fields opposite and generally helped around to finalize any last-minute arrangements. As luck would have it, I was asked to sleep next door on the night before the wedding to accommodate Pamela and her family. This gave me a chance to relax and talk to these friendly neighbours who I had got to know and like. Morag could then concentrate on her own daughter's needs and the focus was then concentrated elsewhere, as I felt she was just doing her duty and her heart was not in it really.

My wedding took place at 2.30 March 27th at the Parish Church in Seer Green. The Groom and some guests wore morning dress with white carnations in their button holes. Sylvia was my only bridesmaid. She looked happy and lovely in a pale-orange, long dress and Robert then aged three was my page boy all dressed to the nines and looking fantastic and very proud. With my ivory dress I wore my high heels, carried a small posy of delicate pale-yellow tea rosebuds. Make up was sparse and my hairstyle kept simple. My groom was almost a foot taller than me and looked so handsome and happy. He had also hired his suit with tails from Moss Brothers and it looked good on his slim, tall figure. He had been given a raucous stag night and his friends gave him mixed alcohol known as Micky Finn and did their best to give him a good send off. Lucky for him he was able to take his drink and just about made it on time and in one piece.

The reception was in a hotel called the White Hart in Beaconsfield. It was buffet style and I don't remember eating a thing. We had a two-tier fruit wedding cake, speeches and telegrams from guests unable to attend. It was all a bit of a whirl and before I knew it, we were saying goodbye to our guests. I packed my dress and gave it to Peter my new brother-in-law and he promised to return it safely to the hire store. I then changed into an oatmeal skirt and jacket with a blue hat, before driving off to spend our honeymoon in the Lake District. We stopped halfway for a meal of fish and chips as we had not eaten much at our reception. I felt somewhat over dressed in my smart going away outfit when we entered the chippie and ate our food wrapped in newspaper which we had sprinkled with salt and vinegar on. Boy we didn't realize we were that hungry and hardly noticed the smell of chips in the car as we continued our journey.

We spent two glorious weeks staying in a hotel overlooking Lake Windermere. The weather was unusually warm for early Spring, we hired walking boots and managed to scale most of the peaks. We had packed lunches washed down with dandelion and burdock, a fizzy drink popular at the time and had an afternoon nap in the sun on some grassy slope. After dinner we would stroll by the lake and watch the sun go down and the moon appear and discuss our future plans. We were happy and excited all at the same time, although we were both young and inexperienced with affairs of the heart – we were determined to give it our best shot! After our honeymoon it was back to Central London to stay at Andrew's parents' flat for three months while our house in Langley was being sorted with the mortgage.

It was straight to work for me cooking, shopping and looking after five adults as there was also a lodger living there too at the time. Gwen was to have a foot operation to correct going on points too early as a child during ballet lessons. She was in hospital for two weeks and the operation helped with her walking. Both Edgar and Andrew were working in London and I generally ran the household and tried to keep shopping within budget as we were saving for the future.

Eventually it was time to move into our house in Langley, an end of terrace with two double bedrooms and a front and back garden. The house was modern with very little character, it was all we could afford at the time and I was delighted to have a house to call my own, also worried about having a mortgage which seemed tremendous at the time. I was not used to owing money and had never been in debt before.

It was also near the M4 where Andrew would commute on his scooter for Peter Lind Construction Company and design the new Post Office Tower in Central London. This was to be a tall building with a revolving restaurant which was novel at the time, there was the opportunity to have a bird's eye view of the capital, while still managing to tuck into a business lunch and to catch the waiter's eye for the bill. I applied for a job at Upton Hospital in Slough as a staff nurse in the General Outpatients' Department. The hours were regular with most weekends off duty. The work was varied with an extremely busy workload of Consultant Appointments covering Diabetes, Orthopaedics, General Medical and Surgical Appointments. I also spent some time learning how to secure Plaster of Paris, a substance used for placing around a splint which had been cut into two for holding together a fractured limb until it had healed. This was a fairly messy procedure and the patients liked to write and draw on their plasters once they had dried out.

I was also riding a scooter now and was able to get to work easily and park behind the hospital. We settled into married life with the odd disagreement in the first year. Andrew was a member of a club in Slough now and was in the water polo team as well as doing competitive swimming. We made a few friends, some from swimming and some from my work. Occasionally we would have dinner parties at the weekends and attend galas together.

On a Friday, I finished work at lunch time, this left time to do the weekly shop and stack it on the scooter rack. I would then head home to do housework to leave the weekend free. It was our usual night to go to the cinema in Slough after supper and it became our end-of-week ritual. We had our mortgage on a joint income, so we therefore decided to delay having children and enjoy some years to be together and take simple holidays camping.

As Andrew was a keen swimmer and looked like a fish while in the water with an effortless front crawl with little splash, he was entered for lots of competitions and often came first. We had our annual holiday in Newquay. This took dedication of at least five hours in the sea surfing to find the perfect wave to ride. It was my time to top up my tan, weather permitting, or get stuck into the latest novel. I was always around in case of accidents, as surfing is not without its dangers. We had an old-fashioned tent which was prone to leaking if wet. The guy ropes were long and anyone passing by too close to the tent could trip over. We cooked on a single calor gas cylinder. We had a beaten-up kettle, tin mugs and metal plates. In the fresh air the meals tasted good despite most coming from packets which needed water added to make them palatable. The two weeks sped by and it was too soon to pack up the tent for another year. It was in my second year of marriage, I decided to complete my second of midwifery training at Upton Hospital in Slough. This would take six months and would require support from Andrew and commitment from me. There was a lot of study and practical work ahead as well as running a house and managing married life to keep it stable and happy for both of us. I like a challenge and was looking forward to it all. Andrew turned out to be helpful and even took to helping a bit around the house.

We were a jolly bunch of girls and I met Ann Monk who was to become a close friend. The midwifery training consisted of practical and time in the classroom for study. We were expected to witness ten normal deliveries before we were allowed to deliver forty that was to be our target. Slough had a large Indian and Pakistan population which could lead to problems with their culture and communication, but on the whole we managed to get over these difficulties well. A larger percentage of babies were born at home in the late 1960's. We were allocated as a midwife and were expected to visit the home of the expectant mother alone and make an assessment of how advanced the labour was, then report back to the midwife if the birth was imminent. All instruments were boiled in the kitchen on the mother's stove and when cool, placed on a sterile cloth ready for use.

When the expectant mother was ready to give birth, you then called the midwife and hoped she would arrive in time. In those days an on-call GP could be called too, if necessary. There was also a group of Obstetrics which could be called in a real emergency called The Flying Squad. These events often took place during the night, I would start up my scooter hoping the neighbours would not be disturbed and set off with delivery packs on the rack. On average there could be three deliveries each night. I was young and fit and dedicated to my chosen profession, all the hard work was enjoyable and kept my mind stimulated. We also visited the new mothers for several days after the birth to check all was well, weighed the baby and gave advice and support with breast feeding. We took a written and practical examination after our six months were completed and we all passed. After eight months working at Upton Hospital in the various maternity departments, Ann Monk and I were called to the Midwifery Matron and asked whether we would like to be promoted to Midwifery Sisters. We were both surprised and accepted with some reservation as we had only practised for the past eight months.

I was set to work on night duty on the labour ward working a twelve-hour shift with no breaks, so it was hectic. I worked with a good Staff Midwife and two registrars who would tackle the more complicated deliveries. All mothers that needed a caesarean operation would go to main theatre. On average we delivered seven normal deliveries each night. It was all I could do to hand over my report to the day staff on the labour ward in a coherent fashion.

On my way home, I stumbled in to a baker's shop to pick up a loaf of bread before collapsing into bed, ready for another busy night. Andrew and I were like passing ships in the night and I left him notes and a prepared meal for him to eat. He appeared not to mind as there were days off and nothing was neglected around the house. We would catch up once I was off-duty and have some form of social life. Andrew was very fond of sport and we had recently bought a television which he enjoyed watching, I was happy just listening to music and plays on the radio at the time.

I was now in charge and working on the post-natal ward as the Ward Sister with thirty mothers and babies. Again, we were short staffed and it was a constant battle to keep the flow of well women to be discharged home before admitting the newly delivered ones. In those days all the babies were nursed in the nursery and attended by a nursery nurse, it was thought this enabled the mothers to rest in between feeding times. Around half chose to breast feed and others bottle fed, a drug representative from a leading brand of formula milk gave us bottles of free samples and these were given to the less well off. I also became friendly with Jenny Cant and her husband Tony. Midwifery was not really for Jenny and after she married Tony, she decided to help him run his carpet and furnishing shop in Slough, which was to be a well-run business for years. I also kept in touch with Ann Monk and her husband Tony. He was a local architect and Andrew and Tony had a lot in common as Andrew could give advice on some of the structural work required for new buildings that Tony was designing. My time at Upton Hospital was coming to an end, it had been a very busy period with numerous deliveries under my belt and was my privilege to care for so many mothers and their lovely babies.

This chapter of my life will stop here. I then went on to work as a midwife and eventually retired at aged 75 years. I travelled to USA mainly on holidays to visit Sylvia who had married a doctor who specialised as an anaesthetist and they eventually settled in Ann Arbor, Michigan and had three children. We are still close friends and we usually meet up each year to help each other through the various challenging events that living does to us. I worked in Dubai before it became a wealthy oil state and lived there with my family, Andrew and two daughters. I lived in Tanzania and Malawi where Andrew was working on projects After a challenging start, my life turned out well and I consider myself as being so lucky. What goes around comes around and there is always time to be kind and spread a little happiness.

Printed in Poland
by Amazon Fulfillment
Poland Sp. z o.o., Wrocław